SO YOU WANT TO GROW A PIE?

BY BRIDGET HEOS • ILLUSTRATED BY DANIELE FABBRI

AMICUS ILLUSTRATED • AMICUS INK

Amicus Illustrated and Amicus Ink
are imprints of Amicus
P.O. Box 1329
Mankato, MN 56002

Library of Congress Cataloging-in-Publication Data
Heos, Bridget, author.
 So you want to grow a pie? / by Bridget Heos ; illustrated by Daniele Fabbri.
    pages cm. — (Grow your food)
 Summary: "A young girl wants to grow her own pie, learns where the many ingredients come from, and grows a fruit tree. Includes kid-friendly apple pie recipe"—Provided by publisher.
 ISBN 978-1-60753-739-7 (library binding)
 ISBN 978-1-60753-906-3 (ebook)
 ISBN 978-1-68152-012-4 (paperback)
1. Apples—Juvenile literature. 2. Fruit trees—Juvenile literature. 3. Pies—Juvenile literature. 4. Gardening—Juvenile literature. I. Fabbri, Daniele, 1978- illustrator. II. Title. III. Series: Heos, Bridget. Grow your food.
 SB363.H424 2016
 634—dc23   2014041495

Editor: Rebecca Glaser
Designer: Kathleen Petelinsek

Printed in the United States of America at Corporate Graphics in North Mankato, Minnesota.

HC 10 9 8 7 6 5 4 3 2 1
PB 10 9 8 7 6 5 4 3 2 1

ABOUT THE AUTHOR

Bridget Heos is the author of more than 70 books for children, including *Mustache Baby* and *Mustache Baby Meets His Match*. She has had a garden since fifth grade and is currently growing tomato sauce and pumpkin and cherry pie. You can find out more about her at www.authorbridgetheos.com.

ABOUT THE ILLUSTRATOR

Daniele Fabbri was born in Ravenna, Italy, in 1978. He graduated from Istituto Europeo di Design in Milan, Italy, and started his career as a cartoon animator, storyboarder, and background designer for animated series. He has worked as a freelance illustrator since 2003, collaborating with international publishers and advertising agencies.

Mmm . . . pies. There are so many flavors. Have you ever wondered where they come from? Many pie ingredients come from plants. You could even grow a pie at home.

Of course you can't grow a whole pie at once.

But you can grow the ingredients.

For the crust you'll need flour, which comes from wheat. And you'll need butter, which comes from cows.

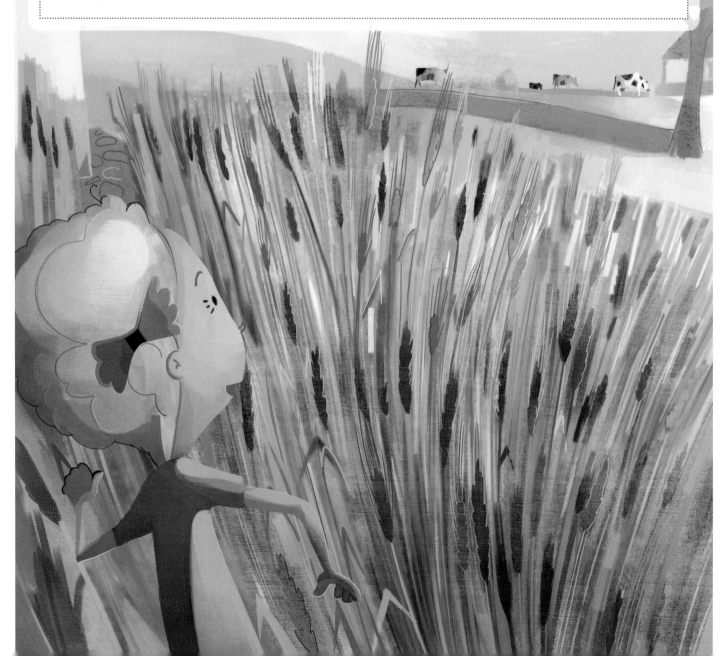

For the pie filling, you'll need to plant sugar cane.

For meringue filling, you need eggs . . .
which means you'll need a chicken coop.

Do you have enough room for all of this?
Probably not unless you live on a farm!

Start with one main ingredient—the fruit. What kind of fruit tree would you like to plant? Before you decide, you should know that different fruits like different climates.

For example, lemons, coconuts, and bananas only like warm weather. And if you live up north, your winters are always cold.

Let's say you live in a warm climate, and want to plant a lemon seed. Wait! Don't plant the seed right in the ground.

The seed is a baby plant. And just as human babies sleep in cradles, a seed starts out in a small container. When it sprouts and grows bigger, you can plant it in the ground.

Water and wait, and wait, and wait. It takes a while for a tree to grow. And it can take a few years for the fruit to grow.

But if you're patient, it will happen. Uh-oh. Are those limes? Nope! The lemons just aren't ripe yet. When they turn yellow, you can squeeze out the lemon juice for your pie!

What if your climate is cold in the winter?
Peaches can grow in cold or hot climates.

And apple and cherry trees actually prefer cold winters. They help the fruit to grow.

An apple tree is a great choice! But unless your neighbor has an apple tree, you'll need two. An apple tree needs a partner. Pollen from two trees has to mix for apples to grow.

Apple trees start out as seeds, too. But people often plant young trees called saplings instead. You'll still have to wait a long time for the apples to grow!

Apples are harvested in fall. When the apples are full size and their true color, it's time to pick them.

Then, slice the fruit for your pie. Mix it with cinnamon and sugar. Add it to the crust. And bake it!

Any way you slice it, it's pie time!

MAKE YOUR OWN APPLE PIE

INGREDIENTS

- 2 unbaked pie crusts (which you can make or buy)
- 7 apples, sliced thinly
- ⅔ cup (165 mL) sugar
- 2 tsp (10 mL) cinnamon
- ¼ cup (65 mL) flour
- 2 Tbsp (30 mL) butter

WHAT YOU DO

1. Heat oven to 425°F (218°C).
2. Mix the sugar, cinnamon, and flour.
3. Place one unbaked pie crust in a pie plate.
4. Add the sliced apples.
5. Pour the cinnamon-sugar mixture evenly over the apples.
6. Slice the butter and place it on top of the apples.
7. Add the other pie crust over the apples. Pinch the edges. With a knife, slice openings in the crust. (You can also use a cookie cutter and cut out shapes.)
8. Bake the pie for 40 to 50 minutes, or until the pie crust is golden brown.

GLOSSARY

climate The weather in one place over a long period of time.

harvest To pick vegetables, fruit, or other plants that are ready to be used.

sapling A baby tree.

seed The part of a plant that produces new plants.

sprout To push up from underground.

weather The condition of the air (temperature, wind, and moisture) at any given time.

READ MORE

Bodden, Valerie. **Apple. Grow with Me**. Mankato, Minn.: Creative Education, 2014.

Stewart, Melissa. **How Does a Seed Sprout?: And Other Questions about Plants**. New York: Sterling, 2014.

Tuminelly, Nancy. **Let's Cook with Apples! : Delicious & Fun Apple Dishes Kids Can Make**. Minneapolis: ABDO, 2013.

WEBSITES

KidsGardening: Helping Young Minds Grow
www.kidsgardening.org
The National Gardening Association has tips on how to start a garden at home or at school.

The Life of a Tree
www.arborday.org/kids/carly/lifeofatree
Learn about how a tree grows and see what the inside of a tree trunk looks like.

My First Garden: A Children's Guide
urbanext.illinois.edu/firstgarden
Learn about the world of fun and clever gardening with step-by-step information on how to start a garden.

Every effort has been made to ensure that these websites are appropriate for children. However, because of the nature of the Internet, it is impossible to guarantee that these sites will remain active indefinitely or that their contents will not be altered.